LOOKING AT LITERATURE

MY FIRST LOOK AT POETRY

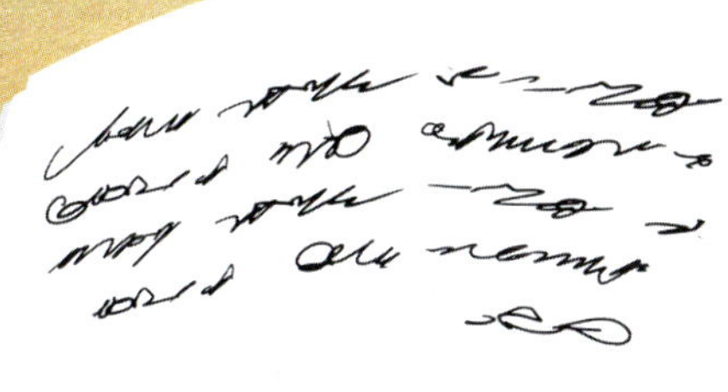

BY ROSIE BANKS

Please visit our website, www.garethstevens.com. For a free color catalog of all our high-quality books, call toll free 1-800-542-2595 or fax 1-877-542-2596.

Library of Congress Cataloging-in-Publication Data

Names: Banks, Rosie, 1978- author.
Title: My first look at poetry / Rosie Banks.
Description: New York : Gareth Stevens Publishing, [2022] | Series: Looking at literature | Includes index.
Identifiers: LCCN 2020029581 (print) | LCCN 2020029582 (ebook) | ISBN 9781538264072 (library binding) | ISBN 9781538264058 (paperback) | ISBN 9781538264065 (6 pack) | ISBN 9781538264089 (ebook)
Subjects: LCSH: Poetry–Juvenile literature.
Classification: LCC PN1031 .B226 2022 (print) | LCC PN1031 (ebook) | DDC 808.1–dc23
LC record available at https://lccn.loc.gov/2020029581
LC ebook record available at https://lccn.loc.gov/2020029582

Published in 2022 by
Gareth Stevens Publishing
111 East 14th Street, Suite 349
New York, NY 10003

Designer: Rachel Rising
Editor: Kate Mikoley

Photo credits: Cover, p. 1 bearsky23/Shutterstock.com; Cover, p. 1 Larissa Kulik/Shutterstock.com; Cover, p.1 Dmitry Karlov/Shutterstock.com; pp. 3, 4, 6, 8, 10, 12, 14, 16, 18, 20, 21, 22, 23, 24 (background) carduus/DigitalVision Vectors/Getty Images; p. 5 Hispanolistic/ E+/Getty Images; p. 7 Joe Raedle/Staff/Getty Images News/Getty Images; p. 8 Culture Club/Contributor/Hulton Archive/Getty Images; p. 9 quiLie/Moment/Getty Images; p. 10 https://en.wikipedia.org/wiki/Robert_Louis_Stevenson#/media/File:Robert_Louis_Stevenson_at_26.jpg; p. 11 Abstract Aerial Art/DigitalVision/Getty Images; p.12 https://commons.wikimedia.org/wiki/File:Natsume_Soseki_photo.jpg; p. 13 Shobeir Ansari/Moment/Getty Images; p. 14 duncan1890/E+/Getty Images; p. 15 Hulton Archive/Stringer/Hulton Fine Art Collection/Getty Images; p. 16 Lisa Larsen/Contributor/The LIFE Picture Collection/Getty Images; p. 17 lisegagne/E+/Getty Images; p. 19 Print Collector/Contributor/Hulton Archive/Getty Images; p. 20 Monica Morgan/Contributor/WireImage/Getty Images; p. 21 Sappington Todd/Getty Images.

Printed in the United States of America

CPSIA compliance information: Batch #CSGS22: For further information contact Gareth Stevens, New York, New York at 1-800-542-2595.

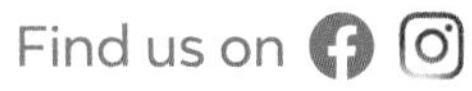

CONTENTS

Boldface words appear in the glossary.

Puzzling Poetry

Poetry is a kind of writing. It's hard to say exactly what it is! Poems can look and sound different. Some **rhyme**, but some don't. Some are long. Others are short. Some tell stories. Others are **descriptions**. Some poems are serious, and some are funny!

Listening to Poems

Rhythm is a **pattern** of sounds. It's like the beat of a song. Many poems have rhythm. It's easy to hear when they're read aloud. A poem's rhythm is called its meter. Dr. Seuss books often have poetry with meter.

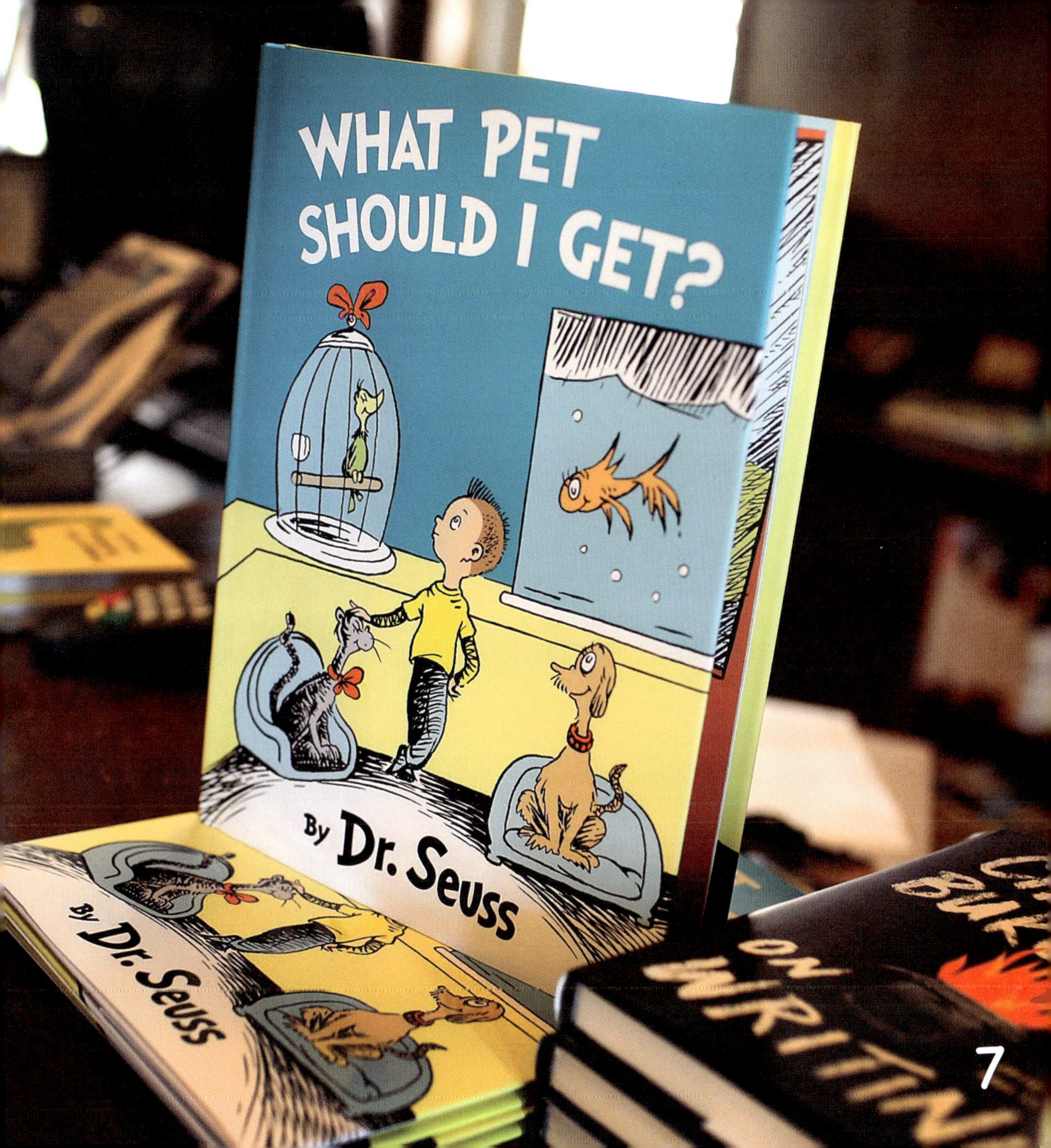
WHAT PET
SHOULD I GET?
By Dr. Seuss
By Dr. Seuss

The meter, or rhythm, of a poem comes from its words. Words are made up of bits called **syllables**. Some syllables are **stressed**. Some aren't. Read the poem on the next page aloud. Listen to the rhythm the syllables create.

Christina Rossetti

Mix a Pancake

by Christina Rossetti

Mix a pancake,
Stir a pancake,
Pop it in the pan;
Fry the pancake,
Toss the pancake—
Catch it if you can.

Looking at Poems

Poetry often looks different than other writing. Words are **arranged** in lines of a certain length. A line of poetry is called a verse. Sometimes, there's just one word in a line! A group of lines in a poem is called a stanza.

Robert Louis Stevenson

At the Sea-Side

by Robert Louis Stevenson

When I was down beside the sea
A wooden spade they gave to me
To dig the sandy shore.

My holes were empty like a cup.
In every hole the sea came up,
Till it could come no more.

Kinds of Poems

Certain kinds of poems have special names. These poems follow a set of rules. A haiku (HY-koo) has three lines. The first and third lines have five syllables each. The second line has seven syllables. Haiku often don't rhyme. Haiku poetry came from Japan.

Natsume Sōseki

Over The Wintry

by Natsume Sōseki

Over the wintry
forest, winds howl in rage
with no leaves to blow.

A sonnet is a poem with 14 lines. It often has rhymes. In the late 1500s and early 1600s, William Shakespeare wrote many sonnets. In the 1800s, Edward Lear wrote funny poems with five lines. These are called limericks. Limericks have a special rhyming pattern.

Shakespeare

There Was an Old Man with a Beard

by Edward Lear

There was an Old Man with a beard,
Who said, "It is just as I feared!—
Two Owls and a Hen,
four Larks and a Wren,
Have all built their nests in my beard."

Some poetry has no rhymes. It's called blank verse. Poetry without rhymes or a regular pattern of rhythm is called free verse. It sounds more like how people speak. However, free verse uses more **imaginative** ideas than normal speaking.

William Carlos Williams

The Red Wheelbarrow

by William Carlos Williams

so much depends
upon

a red wheel
barrow

glazed with rain
water

beside the white
chickens

Ancient Poetry

Poetry is a very old form of writing. It was an easy way to remember stories before people could write. A long poem called the *Epic of Gilgamesh* is more than 4,000 years old! It's about a king in ancient **Mesopotamia**.

Children's Poetry

The best way to learn more about poetry is to read it! The people who write poetry are called poets. Poets Shel Silverstein, Nikki Giovanni, and Naomi Shihab Nye are famous for their poems for young people. Read some, and write your own poems!

Nikki Giovanni

Your Turn!

Think of something you'd like to write a poem about. Decide if you want your poem to have rhymes or meter. Read your poem to a friend.

GLOSSARY

arrange: to put something in a certain order or place

description: a statement that tells someone how something or someone looks

imaginative: having to do with a new or interesting idea

Mesopotamia: a part of Asia between the Tigris and Euphrates Rivers

pattern: the way something happens over and over again

rhyme: to end in the same sound as another word, such as the words cave and wave. Also, a word that has the same ending sound as another word.

stress: to give a syllable in a word a certain force or loudness

syllable: an individual sound that makes up a word in spoken language

FOR MORE INFORMATION

BOOKS

Alarcón, Francisco X. *Family Poems for Every Day of the Week/ Poemas Familiares para Cada Dia de la Semana.* San Francisco, CA: Children's Book Press, 2017.

Pearson, Yvonne. *12 Great Tips on Writing Poetry.* Mankato, MN: 12-Story Library, 2017.

Slade, Suzanne. *Exquisite: The Poetry and Life of Gwendolyn Brooks.* New York, NY: Abrams Books for Young Readers, 2020.

WEBSITES

Children's Poetry
www.poetryfoundation.org/learn/children
Read some poems written especially for young people.

The Kids Are All Write: How to Write a Poem
kidlit.tv/2017/05/the-kids-are-all-write-how-to-write-a-poem/
Follow these tips for writing your own poem.

Publisher's note to educators and parents: Our editors have carefully reviewed these websites to ensure that they are suitable for students. Many websites change frequently, however, and we cannot guarantee that a site's future contents will continue to meet our high standards of quality and educational value. Be advised that students should be closely supervised whenever they access the Internet.

INDEX